Introduction

What is an heirloom?

An heirloom is a treasure, something cherished for its beauty, its uniqueness or its charm.

No matter how many afghans you make, there will always be one that will stand out in your mind; one that you know will be cherished and passed down in your family for generations to come; one that you make over and over again as a special gift for many occasions.

Perhaps you will find your special afghan in this unusual collection.

What makes the collection special is the use of borders — wonderful borders that add an elegant touch to make the afghan a truly memorable one.

We know you will enjoy making these beauties.

Credits

Carol Wilson Mansfield, Photo Stylist,
Wayne Norton, Photography
Graphic Solutions, inc-chgo, Book Design
Created by The Creative Partners™

All the afghans in this book were tested to ensure the accuracy and clarity of the instructions. We are grateful to the following pattern testers:

Kim Britt
Sharon Butcher
Carrie Cristiano
Vinette De Phillipe
Patricia Honaker
Debra Hughes
Jennie Lute
Bonnie Pierce
Kelly Robinson

Every effort has been made to ensure the accuracy of these instructions. We cannot be responsible for human error or variations in your work.

A Note on Yarns

Whenever we have used a specialty yarn, we have given the brand name. If you are unable to find these yarns locally, write to the following manufacturers who will be able to tell you where to purchase their products, or consult their internet sites. We also wish to thank these companies for supplying yarn for this book:

Bernat Yarns
320 Livingston Avenue South
Listowel, Ontario
Canada N4W 3H3
www. Bernat.com

Red Heart Yarns
Coats and Clark
Consumer Services
P.O. Box 12229
Greenville, South Carolina 29612-0229

TLC Yarns
Coats and Clark
Consumer Services
P.O.Box 12229
Greenville, South Carolina 29612-0229
www.Coatsandclark.com

Abbreviations & Symbols

sc	single crochet
hdc	half double crochet
dc	double crochet
tr	triple crochet
dtr	double triple crochet
tr tr	triple triple crochet
ch(s)	chain(s)
sl st	slip stitch
beg	begin(ning)
CL(s)	cluster(s)
cont	continue
inc	increase
lp(s)	loop(s)
patt	pattern
prev	previous
rem	remaining
rep	repeat(ing)
rnd(s)	round(s)
sk	skip
sl	slip
sp(s)	space(s)
st(s)	stitches
sp(s)	space(s)
st(s)	stitch(es)
tog	together
YO	yarn over

* An asterisk (or double asterisks**) in a pattern row, indicates a portion of instructions to be used more than once. For instance, "rep from * three times" means that after working the instructions once, you must work them again three times for a total of 4 times in all.

† A dagger (or double daggers††) indicates those instructions that will be repeated again later in the same row or round.

: The number after a colon tells you the number of stiches you will have when you have completed the row or round.

( ) Parentheses enclose instructions which are to be worked the number of times following the parentheses. For instance, "(ch1, sc, ch 1) 3 times" means that you will chain one, work one sc, and then chain once again three times for a total of six chains and 3 sc.

Parentheses often set off or clarify a group of stitches to be worked into the same space or stitch. For instance, "(dc, ch2, dc) in corner sp."

[ ] Brackets and ( ) parentheses are also used to give you additional information.

Terms

Front Loop—This is the loop toward you at the top of the stitch.

Back Loop—This is the loop away from you at the top of the stitch.

Post—This is the vertical part of the stitch.

Join—This means to join with a sl st unless another stitch is specified.

Finish Off—This means to end your piece by pulling the yarn through the last loop remaining on the hook, then cutting the yarn. This will prevent the work from unraveling.

Work Even—This means that the work is continued in the pattern as established without increasing or decreasing.

Continue in Pattern as Established—This means to follow the pattern stitch as it has been set up, working any increases or decreases in such a way that the pattern remains the same as it was established.

Gauge

It is extremely important that your personal gauge matches the gauge given in the pattern. Otherwise you may not have enough yarn to complete your afghan. Crochet a swatch that is about 4" square, using the suggested hook and number of stitches given in the pattern. Measure your swatch. If the number of stitches are fewer than those listed in the pattern, try making another swatch with a smaller hook. If the number of stitches are more than are called for in the pattern, try making another swatch with a larger hook.

Terms which may have different equivalents...

The afghan patterns in this book have been written using the crochet terminology that is used in the United States. Terms which may have different equivalents in other parts of the world are listed below.

United States	International
Slip stitch (sl st)	single crochet (sc)
Single crochet (sc)	double crochet (dc)
Half double crochet (hdc)	half treble crochet (htr)
Double crochet (dc)	treble crochet (tr)
Triple crochet (trc)	double treble crochet (dtr)
Skip	miss
Gauge	tension
Yarn over (YO)	Yarn over hook (YOH)

Crochet Hooks

US	B-1	C-2	D-3	E-4	F-5	G-6	H-8	I-9	J-10	K-10½	N	P	Q
Metric	2.25	2.75	3.25	3.5	3.75	4	5	5.5	6	6.5	9	10	15

Bullion Fans
designed by Bonnie Pierce

This afghan is truly a treasure! The deeply dimensional fans, worked in bullion stitches, add an elegant touch. If you are not familiar with working bullions, you'll enjoy learning a new skill. Mastering the stitch takes a little patience and a little practice, but the result is well worth the effort.

Learning the Bullion Stitch

If you've never done the bullion st before, you'll want to practice before starting the afghan. The bullion stitch is basically like a hdc, but with a lot more yarn overs. To practice, work this sample swatch with scrap yarn.

Ch 11.

Row 1: Sc in 2nd ch from hook and in each rem ch: 10 sc; ch 3 (counts as first st of following row). Turn.

Row 2: YO, insert hook in next sc and draw up a lp; YO and draw through all 3 lps on hook. You have now made one hdc.

For the next st, YO twice, insert hook in next sc and draw up a lp, YO and draw through all 4 lps on hook (**Diagram 1**).

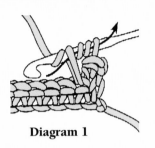

Diagram 1

Bullion Fans

Size
48" x 56"

Materials
Worsted weight yarn,
    46 oz white
    Note: Photographed model made with
    Red Heart® Classic™ #1 White
Size I (5.5 mm) crochet hook
    (or size required for gauge)

Gauge
17 sts = 6"
2 rows = 1"

Stitch Guide

Bullion St: YO 10 times, insert hook in next st and draw up a lp, YO and draw through all 12 lps on hook.

Bullion Fan St: (Bullion st, ch 1) 5 times in specified st.

2 sc tog: This is a decrease; to work, (insert hook in next sc and draw up a lp) twice, YO and draw through all 3 lps on hook: dec made.

Try to draw through all 4 lps at once, but if you need to, you can use your fingers to pull the lps off carefully one at a time. You have made a 2-YO bullion st.

For the next st, YO 3 times, insert hook in next sc and draw up a lp, YO and draw through all 5 lps on hook. You have made a 3-YO bullion st (**Diagram 2**).

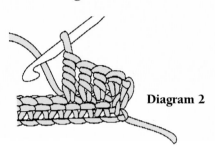

Diagram 2

Continue in this manner across, adding one more YO at the beginning of each st, until you have 10 YOs.

The 10-YO bullion st is the one we are using in this afghan.

Five bullions with a ch-1 after each bullion are worked together in the same st to create a Bullion Fan.

Instructions

Ch 137.

Row 1 (wrong side): Sc in 2nd chain from hook and in each rem ch: 136 sc; ch 3 (counts as first st of following row), turn.

Row 2: Skip next 2 sc, Bullion Fan St in next sc, skip 3 sc, sc in next sc; *skip next 3 sc, Bullion Fan in next sc, skip 3 sc, sc in next sc; rep from * across to last 4 sts, skip 3 sc, dc in last sc: 17 Bullion Fans made; ch 1, turn.

Row 3: Sc in dc, *(2 sc in ch 1 sp between bullions) four times, sc in next sc; rep from * across, ending sc in 3rd ch of beg ch, ch 4 (counts as a dc and ch-1 sp), turn.

Row 4: (Bullion, ch 1) twice in first sc, skip 3 sc; *sc in next 2 sc, skip 3 sc, Bullion Fan in next sc, skip 3 sc; rep from *across to last st, in last st work (bullion, ch 1) twice, dc in same sc; ch 1, turn.

Row 5: Sc in dc, skip next ch-1 sp, 2 sc in next ch -1 sp between bullions;* 2 sc tog, (2 sc in next ch 1 sp between bullions) 4 times; rep from * across, ending 2 sc in ch -1 sp between bullions, sc in 3rd ch of beg ch, ch 3, turn.

Row 6: Skip next 3 sts; *Bullion Fan in next st, skip 3 sts, sc in next 2 sts, skip 3 sts; rep from * across to last 5 sts, ending Bullion Fan in next st, skip 3 sts, sc in 3rd ch of beg ch, ch 1, turn.

Row 7: Sc in first sc, *(2 sc in next ch-1 sp between bullions) 4 times, 2 sc tog; rep from * across, ending sc in 3rd ch of beg ch, ch 3, turn.

Rep Rows 4 through 7 for a total of 55 bullion rows (110 rows in all); at end of last row, do not ch 3, finish off. Weave in ends.

Sign of Spring
designed by Jean Leinhauser

Those first pale green leaf buds that appear in early spring are filled with promise, and this afghan promises you a beautiful way to keep warm.

Size
48½" x 50" before borders

Materials
Worsted weight yarn,
48 oz green
  Note: Photographed model made with TLC® Essentials™ #2672 Light Thyme
Size H (5mm) crochet hook
  (or size required for gauge)

Gauge
7 dc = 2"
1 dc row = ¾"

Stitch Guide

Double Cluster (Dcl): (YO, insert hook in next st and draw up a lp to height of a dc) 4 times, YO and draw through all 9 lps on hook, ch 3; (YO, insert hook in same st and draw up a lp) 4 times, YO and draw through all 9 lps: Dcl made.

Instructions
Ch 170.

Row 1: Sc in 2nd ch from hook and in each rem ch: 169 sc; ch 3 (counts as a dc here and throughout pattern), turn.

Row 2 (right side): Dc in next 2 sc; *skip next sc, Dcl in next sc, skip next sc, dc in next 2 sc; rep from * across, ending last rep with dc in last 3 sc; ch 1, turn.

Row 3: Sc in first 3 dc, 3 sc in ch-3 lp of next Dcl; *sc in next 2 dc, 3 sc in ch-3 lp of next Dcl; rep from * across, ending last rep sc in last 3 dc; ch 3, turn.

Row 4: Dc in each sc, ch 1, turn.

Row 5: Sc in each dc, ch 3, turn.

Rep Rows 2 through 5 until work measures about 49", then rep Rows 2 and 3 once more. At end of last row, ch 1 instead of 3, turn.

Edging
Rnd 1: 3 sc for corner in first st; work sc around outer edge of afghan, working 3 sc in each outer corner, and adjusting sts to keep work flat; join with a sl st in beg sc, finish off, weave in ends.

Top Border
Hold afghan with right side facing and one short end at top; Join yarn in center sc of 3-sc corner group at top right.

Row 1: Ch 1, sc in same st; *ch 3, skip next 2 sc, sc in next sc; rep from * across; ch 5, turn.

Row 2: Sc in next sc; *ch 5, sc in next sc; rep from * across; ch 7, turn.

Row 3: Sc in next sc; *ch 7, sc in next sc; rep from * across; ch 5, turn.

Row 4: Dc in front of ch-7 lp of Row 3 and into ch-5 lp of Row 2 ; ch 5, sc in next sc; *ch 5, dc in front of ch-7 and into ch-5 lp as before, ch 5, sc in next sc; rep from * across; ch 5, turn.

Row 5: (Dc, ch 3, dc) in next dc; ch 5, sc in next sc; * ch 5, (dc, ch 3, dc) in next dc; ch 5, sc in next sc; rep from * across; ch 1, turn.

Row 6: *5 sc in next ch-5 lp, (2 dc, ch 3, 2 dc) in next ch-3 lp; 5 sc in next ch-5 lp; rep from * across, sc in last st; finish off.

Bottom Border
Work as for Top Border across opposite short end of afghan.

Blue on Blue

designed by Jean Leinhauser

This wonderful afghan is a true masterpiece, from its center with little chain loops to the unusual and elegant border.

Size

44" x 54" before border

Materials

Worsted weight yarn,

    51 oz medium blue

    7 oz pale blue

    Note: Photographed model made with Bernat® Berella® "4" #1142 True Periwinkle Blue and #1143 Soft Periwinkle Blue

Size H (5mm) crochet hook

    (or size required for gauge)

Gauge

7 dc = 2"

Instructions

With medium blue, ch 148.

Row 1: Sc in 2nd ch from hook and in each rem ch: 147 sc; ch 3 (counts as first dc of following row here and throughout pattern), turn.

Row 2: Dc in each sc, ch 3, turn.

Row 3: Dc in each dc and in 3rd ch of beg ch, ch 3, turn.

Row 4: Dc in each dc, and in 3rd ch of beg ch, ch 1, turn.

Row 5: (right side): Sc in first 2 dc; * ch 6, sc in next dc; rep from * across to last 2 sts, sc in last dc; and in 3rd ch of beg; ch 3, turn.

Row 6: Dc in first sc;* working behind ch-6 lps of Row 5, dc in each sc; ch 3, turn.

Row 7: Dc in each dc, ch 3, turn.

Row 8: Dc in each dc, ch 1, turn.

Rep Rows 5 through 8 until piece measures about 54" from beg ch, ending by working a Row 8.

Border

Rnd 1 (right side): 3 sc in first dc for first corner; work sc around outer edge of afghan, working 3 sc in each outer corner, and adjusting sts to keep work flat; join with a sl st in beg sc, finish off medium blue.

Rnd 2: Join light blue with sc in last st; *ch 8, skip 4 sc, sc in next sc; rep from * around (note: at end of rnd, you may need to skip 3 or 5 sc instead of 4 to come out even); join in beg sc.

Rnd 3: Ch 1, sc in first sc; *in next ch-8 lp work shell of (sc, hdc, 2 dc, tr, ch 3, tr, 2 dc, hdc, sc); sc in next center sc; rep from * around, join in beg sc.

Rnd 4: Ch 1, sc in first sc; *ch 6; in ch-3 sp at top of next shell work (dc, ch 3, dc); ch 6, sc in next sc; rep from * around, join in beg sc.

Rnd 5: Ch 1, sc in first sc; *6 sc in next ch-6 sp, (sc, ch 3, sc) in ch-3 sp at top of shell; 6 sc in next ch-6 sp, sc in next sc; rep from * around, join in beg sc, finish off. Weave in all ends.

Marvelous in Mauve

designed by Jean Leinhauser

*Delicate fans are accented by cluster stitches in this pretty throw,
with a lavish lacy border on all four sides.*

Size

43" x 59" before border

Materials

Worsted weight yarn,

    39 oz mauve

    Note: Photographed model made with
Bernat® Berella® "4" #1305 Soft Mauve

Size H (5mm) crochet hook

    (or size required for gauge)

Gauge

7 dc = 2"

Stitch Guide

Cluster (CL): Keeping last lp of each dc on
hook, 3 dc in st indicated; YO and draw
through all 4 lps on hook: CL made.

Double Cluster (DCL): Keeping last lp
of each dc on hook, dc in next dc, skip next
CL, dc in next dc; YO and draw through all
3 lps on hook: DCL made.

Instructions

Ch 154.

Row 1: 2 dc in 4th ch from hook, ch 3, skip
next 4 chs, sc in next ch; ch 3, skip next 4
chs, * 5 dc in next ch; ch 3, skip next 4 chs,
sc in next ch; ch 3, skip next 4 chs; rep
from * to last ch, 3 dc in last ch: 180 sts
(counting beg 3 skipped chs as a dc); ch 4
(counts as first dc and ch-1 sp on next row),
turn.

Row 2 (right side): (Dc in next dc, ch 1)
twice; CL (see Stitch Guide) in next sc, ch 1;
* (dc in next dc, ch 1) 5 times; CL in next sc,
ch 1; rep from * to last 3 sts; (dc in next dc,
ch 1) twice; dc in 3rd ch of beg 3 skipped chs
ch 5 (counts as first dc and ch-2 sp of
following row), turn.

Row 3: Dc in next dc, ch 2; DCL (see Stitch Guide), ch 2; * (dc in next dc, ch 2) 3 times; DCL, ch 2; rep from * to last dc, dc in last dc; ch 2, sk next ch of turning ch 5, dc in next ch; ch 1, turn.

Row 4: Sc in first dc, ch 1; *sc in next ch-2 sp, ch 3; rep from * to turning ch, sk next ch, sc in next ch; ch 3, turn.

Row 5: 2 dc in first sc; ch 3, skip next ch-3 sp, sc in next ch-3 sp, ch 3, ski[next ch-3 sp; *5 dc in next ch-3 sp; ch 3, skip next ch-3 sp, sc in next ch-3 sp, ch 3, skip next ch-3 sp; rep from * to last 2 sc, skip next sc, 3 dc in last sc; ch 3, turn.

Rep Rows 2 through 5 until piece measures about 59", ending by working a Row 4. At end of last row, do not work ch-3, finish off.

Border

Hold afghan with right side facing you and last row at top; join yarn with a sl st in first st at upper right corner.

Rnd 1: Ch 1, 3 sc in same st (first corner made); sc in each st across row to last st, work 3 sc in last st for 2nd corner; work sc around entire outer edge, working 3 sc in each outer corner, and adjusting sts to keep work flat; join in beg sc.

Rnd 2: Sl st in next sc; (ch 3, 3 dc, ch 3, 4 dc) in same sc; *skip next 2 sc, 4 dc in next sc; rep from * to next corner 3-sc group, in center sc work (4 dc, ch 3, 4 dc); rep from * around, join in 3rd ch of beg ch-3.

Rnd 3: Sl st in next dc , (ch 4, dc) in same dc *(dc, ch 1 dc) in next dc; rep from * around, working (dc, ch 1, dc) twice in each ch-3 sp; join in 3rd ch of beg ch-4.

Rnd 4: *Sc in next ch-1 sp, ch 5, sc in next ch-1 sp; ch 10; rep from * around, join in beg sc.

Finish off, weave in ends.

A Touch of Frost
designed by Jean Leinhauser

Crisp and bright as an early frost, this striking afghan is accented with double rows of loopy fringe at each end. Vertical columns of post stitches add texture.

Size

51" x 64" before borders

Materials

Worsted weight yarn,

    84 oz white

    Note: Photographed model made with

    Caron® Simply Soft® #9701 White

Size H (5mm) crochet hook

    (or size required for gauge)

Gauge

7 dc = 2"

Stitch Guide

Back Post dc (BPdc): YO, insert hook from back to front to back around post (vertical bar) of specified dc, YO, draw through first 2 lps, YO and draw through rem lps: BPdc made.

Front Post dc (FPdc): YO, insert hook from front to back to front around post (vertical bar) of specified dc, YO, draw through first 2 lps, YO and draw through rem lps: FPdc made.

Shell: (2 dc, ch 1, 2 dc) in specified st or lp.

BLO: Work in back lp only of specified st.

Instructions

Loosely ch 182.

Row 1: Sc in 2nd ch from hook and in each rem ch: 181 sc; ch 3 (counts as first dc of following row), turn.

Row 2 (right side)**:** Dc in next 4 sc; *sk next sc, in next sc work shell of (2 dc, ch 1, 2 dc); sk next sc, dc in next 3 sc; rep from * to last 5 sts, dc in last 5 sc; ch 3 (counts as first dc of following row), turn.

Row 3: BPdc in next 4 dc; *shell in ch-1 lp of next shell, sk next 2 dc of shell, BPdc in next 3 dc; rep from * across to last 5 dc, BPdc in next 4 dc, dc in 3rd ch of beg; ch 3, turn.

Row 4: FPdc in next 4 dc; *shell in ch-1 sp of next shell, FPdc in next 3 sts; rep from * to last 5 sts, FPdc in next 4 sts, dc in 3rd ch of beg ch; ch 3, turn.

Rep Rows 3 and 4 until piece measures about 64", ending by working a Row 3. At end of last row, ch 1 instead of 3, turn.

Next Row: Sc in first 5 dc; *sk first 2 dc of shell, 3 sc in ch-1 sp, sk last 2 dc of shell; sc in next 3 dc; rep from * to last 5 sts, dc in last 5 sts. Finish off.

Edging

Hold piece with right side facing you and with last row at top

Rnd 1 (right side)**:** Join yarn with sc in first dc, 2 sc in same st: beg corner made; sc across row, 3 sc in last dc for next corner; continue to sc evenly around outer edges of afghan, working 3 sc in each outer corner; join to beg sc, sl st in next sc.

Top Border

(worked across one short end only)
Row 1 (right side)**:** Ch 1, sc in BLO of each sc across to next 3 sc corner, sc in first and center sc of corner, ch 1, turn.

Row 2: Sc in each sc across, ch 30, turn.

Row 3: Sc in first sc; *ch 30, sc in next sc; rep from * to last sc, (sc, ch 30, sc) in last sc, do not turn; finish off.

Row 4: Hold piece with right side facing you; join yarn with sc in first unused lp of Row 1 at right edge; ch 20, sc in same lp; *ch 20, sc in next lp; rep from * to last lp, in last lp work (sc, ch 20, sc). Finish off.

Bottom Border

Hold piece with right side facing you and opposite short end at top; join yarn with sl st in first sc at right edge.

Rep Rows 1 through 4 of Top border. Finish off, weave in ends.

20

Just Peachy
designed by Jean Leinhauser

Fresh as the bloom on a ripe peach, this afghan begs to be caressed and enjoyed both as a cover and as a room accent. Its graceful border completes the picture.

Size
40" x 50" before border

Materials
Worsted weight yarn,
    42 oz peach
    Note: Photographed model made with
    Caron® Simply Soft® #9737 Lt Country
    Peach
Size H (5mm) crochet hook
    (or size required for gauge)

Gauge
7 dc = 2"

Instructions
Ch 133.

Row 1: Sc in 2nd ch from hook and in each rem ch: 132 sc; ch 3 (counts as first dc of next row throughout), turn.

Row 2 (right side): *Dc in next 4 sc, sk 2 sc, (3 dc, ch 3, 3 dc) in next sc (shell made); skip next 2 sc; rep from * across to last 5 sc, dc in last 5 sc, ch 3, turn.

Row 3: *Dc in next 4 dc, ch 3, sc in ch-3 sp of next shell, ch 3; rep from * across to last 5 dc, dc in last 5 dc; ch 3, turn.

Row 4: Dc in next 4 dc; * (3 dc, ch 3, 3 dc) in next sc, dc in next 4 dc; rep from * across to last 5 dc, dc in last 5 dc, ch 3, turn.

Rep Rows 3 and 4 until piece measures about 50", ending by working a Row 3. At end of last row, ch 1, turn.

Border
Rnd 1(right side): 3 sc in first dc for corner; sc in next 4 dc; *3 sc in ch-3 sp, sc in next sc, 3 sc in ch-3 sp, sc in next 4 dc; rep from * across, ending 3 sc for corner in last dc. Working along side edge, work 2 sc in side of each row, adjusting sts as needed to keep work flat, to beg ch; 3 sc for corner in unused

21

lp of first ch; working in unused lps of beg ch, sc in each lp, work 3 sc for corner; sc up last side as before, join in beg sc.

Rnd 2: Sl st into next sc; (ch 3, 2 dc, ch 3, 3 dc) in same sc for corner; *sk 3 sc, shell of (3 dc, ch 3, 3 dc) in next sc; rep from * around, join with sl st to 3rd ch of beg ch-3.

Rnd 3: Sl st in next 2 dc and into ch-3 sp; (ch 3, 3 dc, ch 3, 4 dc) in same sp; * ch 1; in center sp of next shell work (4 dc, ch 3, 4 dc); rep from * around, join with sl st to 3rd ch of beg ch-3.

Rnd 4: Sl st in next 3 dc and into ch-3 sp; (ch 3, 3 dc, ch 3, 4 dc) in same sp; * ch 2; in center sp of next shell work (4 dc, ch 4, 4 dc); rep from * around, join to 3rd ch of beg ch-3.

Rnd 5: Sl st in next 3 dc and into ch-4 sp; (ch 3, 4 dc, ch 4, 5 dc) in same sp; * ch 3; in center sp of next shell work (5 dc, ch 4, 5 dc); rep from * around, join to 3rd ch of beg ch-3. Finish off, weave in ends.

Summer Sky
designed by Jean Leinhauser

What a perfect day! A clear blue sky with billowing white clouds – this afghan hints of lazy summer days and will keep away an evening chill.

Size
41" x 47" before border

Materials
Worsted weight yarn,
   36 oz light blue
   6 oz white
   Note: Photographed model made with Caron® Simply Soft® #9709 Lt.Country Blue and #9701 White
Size H (5 mm) crochet hook
   (or size required for gauge)

Gauge
7 dc = 2"

Stitch Guide

Cluster St (CL) **:** (YO hook, insert hook in specified st and draw up a lp, YO and draw through first 2 lps on hook) 4 times, YO and draw through all 5 lps on hook: CL made.

Instructions
With blue, ch 144.

Row 1: Sc in 2nd ch from hook and in each rem ch: 143 sc; ch 4 (counts as first dc and ch-1 sp on following row), turn.

Row 2: * Sk next sc, dc in next sc, ch 1; rep from * across, ending dc in last sc; ch 4, turn.

Row 3 (right side)**:** *CL in next dc, ch 1, sk next ch-1 sp; rep from * across, ending dc in 3rd ch of turning ch-4; ch 4, turn.

Row 4: *Dc in next CL, ch 1, sk next ch-1 sp; rep from * across, ending dc in 3rd ch of turning ch-4; ch 4, turn.

Rep Rows 3 and 4 until piece measures about 47" ending by working a Row 4. At end of last row, ch 1, turn,

Next Row: Sc in each dc and in each ch-1 sp across, sc in last dc; finish off.

Border

With right side of piece facing you and beg ch at top, join white yarn with a sl st in first unused lp of beg ch at right upper corner.

Rnd 1: Ch 1, 3 sc in same lp for first corner; sc in each lp to last lp, 3 sc for corner in last lp; continue working sc around all rem edges of afghan, adjusting sts to keep work flat and working 3 sc in each rem outer corner; join with sl st in beg sc.

Rnd 2: Sl st in next sc, ch 1, 3 sc for corner in same sc; work sc in each sc, around, working 3 sc in center st of each rem 3 sc corner group; join with sc in beg sc.

Rnd 3: * Ch 3, sk 2 sc, sc in next sc; rep from * around, join with sl st in beg sc.

Rnd 4: Sl st in next ch-3 sp, work shell of (ch 3, 2 dc, ch 3, 3 dc) in same sp; * sc in next ch-3 sp, shell of (3 dc, ch 3, 3 dc) in next sp; rep from * around, join with sl st in 3rd ch of beg ch-3.

Rnd 5: Sl st in next 2 dc and into ch-3 sp; in same sp work (ch 3, 2 dc, ch 4, 3 dc); *tr in next sc, shell of (3 dc, ch 4, 3 dc) in next ch-3 sp; rep from * around, join in 3rd ch of beg ch-3. Finish off white.

Rnd 6: With right side facing, join blue with sc in any tr of Rnd 5; * in next ch-4 sp work shell of (4 dc, ch 4, 4 dc); sc in next tr; rep from * around, join. Finish off, weave in ends.

Lovely Lace
designed by Denise Black

Truly feminine is this creation with a wonderful, deep border that rivals the look of cherished laces. This would be a wonderful gift for a bride.

Size

33" x 46" before border

Materials

Worsted weight yarn

    42 oz cream

    Note: Photographed model made with TLC® Amoré™ # 3103 Vanilla

Size H (5mm) crochet hook

    (or size required for gauge)

Gauge

7 dc=2"

Instructions

Ch 114.

Row 1 (right side): Dc in 4th ch from hook (beg 3 skipped chs count as a dc), dc in each rem ch: 112 dc; ch 1, turn.

Row 2: In first dc work (sc, 2 dc); * skip next 2 dc, in next dc work (sc, 2 dc); rep from * across to last 3 dc; skip next 2 dc, sc in 3rd ch of beg 3 skipped chs; ch 3 (counts as a dc on following rows), turn.

Row 3: Dc in each st; ch 1, turn.

Rep Rows 2 and 3 until piece measures about 46" long, ending by working a Row 3. At end of last row, finish off.

Border

Hold afghan with right side facing you and last row worked at top; join yarn with sc in first dc in upper right-hand corner.

Rnd 1: For first corner, work 2 sc in same st as joining; work sc around outer edge of afghan, working 3 sc in each outer corner, and adjusting sts to keep work flat; join with a sl st to beg sc; sl st into next sc .

Rnd 2: Ch 6 (counts as first dc and ch-3 sp), dc in same st: beg corner made;* (ch 1, dc in next sc) in each st to center sc of next 3-sc corner group, ch 1; in center sc work (dc, ch 3, dc); rep from * twice more, (ch 1, dc in next sc) in each st to beg corner, ch 1, join with sl st in 3rd ch of beg ch.

Rnd 3: Sl st in ch-3 sp; ch 4 (counts as a dc and ch-1 sp), in same sp work (dc, ch 3, dc,

ch 1, dc); ch 1, *(dc in next ch-1 sp, ch 1) to next corner ch-3 sp; in ch-3 sp work (dc, ch 1, dc, ch 3, dc, ch 1, dc,); ch 1, rep from * twice more; (dc in next ch-1 sp, ch 1) to beg corner, join in 3rd ch of beg ch.

Rnd 4: Sl st in ch-1 sp, ch 4 (counts as a dc and ch-1 sp), in next ch-3 sp work (dc, ch 3, dc); ch 1, *(dc in next ch-1 sp, ch 1) to next corner ch-3 sp; in next sp work (dc, ch 3, dc); ch 1, rep from * twice more; (dc in next ch-1 sp, ch 1) to beg ch-4, join in 3rd ch of beg ch.

Rnd 5: Sl st in next ch-1 sp, ch 4; in next corner ch-3 sp work (dc, ch 1, dc; ch 3, dc, ch 1, dc); ch 1, *(dc in next ch-1 sp, ch 1) to next corner ch-3 sp, in sp work (dc, ch 1, dc; ch 3, dc, ch 1, dc); ch 1, rep from * twice more, (dc in next ch-1 sp, ch 1) to beg ch 4, join in 3rd ch of beg ch.

Rnd 6: Sl st in next ch-1 sp, ch 4; in next ch-1 sp work dc, ch 1; in next ch-3 sp work (dc , ch 3, dc); ch 1. *(dc in next ch-1 sp, ch 1) to next corner ch-3 sp, *in sp work (dc, ch 3, dc); ch 1, rep from * twice more; (dc in next ch-1 sp,ch 1) to beg ch-4, join in 3rd ch of beg ch.

Rnd 7: Sl st in next ch-1 sp, ch 4, dc in next ch-1 sp, ch 1; in next corner ch-3 sp work (dc, ch 1, dc; ch 3, dc, ch 1, dc); ch 1, *(dc in next ch-1 sp, ch 1) to next corner ch-3 sp; in sp work (dc, ch 1, dc; ch 3, dc, ch 1, dc); ch 1, rep from * twice more, (dc in next ch-1 sp, ch 1) to beg ch- 4, join in 3rd ch of beg ch.

Rnd 8: Sl st in next ch-1 sp, ch 4; (dc in next ch-1 sp, ch 1) twice; in next corner ch-3 sp work (dc, ch 1, dc; ch 3, dc, ch 1, dc); ch 1, * (dc in next ch-1 sp, ch 1) to next corner ch-3 sp, in sp work (dc, ch 1, dc; ch 3, dc, ch 1, dc); ch 1, rep from * twice more, (dc in next ch-1 sp, ch 1) to beg ch-4, join in 3rd ch of beg ch.

Rnd 9: Sl st in next ch-1 sp, ch 4, (dc in next ch-1 sp, ch 1) 3 times; in next corner ch-3 sp work (dc, ch 1, dc; ch 3, dc, ch 1, dc); ch 1,* (dc in next ch-1 sp, ch 1) to next corner ch-3 sp, in sp work (dc, ch 1, dc; ch 3, dc, ch 1, dc); ch 1, rep from * twice more, (dc in next ch-1 sp, ch 1) to beg ch-4, join in 3rd ch of beg ch.

Rnd 10: Sl st in next ch-1 sp, ch 4; (dc in next ch-1 sp, ch 1) 4 times; in next corher ch-3 sp work (dc, ch 1, dc; ch 3, dc, ch 1, dc); ch 1, *(dc in next ch-1 sp, ch 1) to next corner ch-3 sp, in sp work (dc, ch 1, dc; ch 3, dc, ch 1, dc); ch 1, rep from * 2 times more, (dc in next ch-1 sp, ch 1) to beg ch-4, join in 3rd ch of beg ch.

Rnd 11: Sl st in next ch-1 sp, ch 1; in same sp work (sc, ch 3, sc in first ch made): picot made; picot in each ch-1 sp to next corner ch-3 sp, 4 picots in ch-3 sp; picot in each ch-1 sp and 4 picots in each corner ch-3 sp around, join in beg sc; finish off, weave in ends.

Wild Rose
designed by Jean Leinhauser

Sweet as wild roses rambling along a country fence, this afghan is fun to make as the roses are worked in as you go. The dimensional flowers are unusual and command attention.

Size
44" x 50" before border

Materials
Worsted weight yarn,
54 oz rose
> *Note:* Photographed model made with TLC® Essentials™ #2772 Light Country Rose

Size H (5mm) crochet hook
> (or size required for gauge)

Gauge
7 dc = 2"

Stitch Guide

Front Post Double Crochet (FPdc):
YO, insert hook from front to back to front around Post (vertical bar) of next dc, draw up a lp; (YO, draw through 2 lps on hook) twice: FPdc made.

Flower Circle (FC):
Work (FPdc, ch 3) 6 times around post of next dc; turn work upside down and work (FPdc, ch 3) 5 times around post of previous dc on same row; work one more FPdc around same post: FC made.

Flower Circle Practice Piece
The Flower Circle is not difficult to do, but you might want to practice it before you start the afghan.
Ch 13.

Row 1: Sc in 2nd ch from hook and in each rem ch: 12 sc; ch 3 (counts as first st of next row), turn.

Row 2: Dc in each sc, ch 3, turn.

Row 3: Dc in each dc, ch 3, turn.

Row 4 (right side): Dc in next 5 dc, work FC around next dc; dc in top of same dc (behind the FC), dc in last 5 dc; ch 3, turn.

Row 5: Dc in each dc; finish off.

Instructions

Ch 157.

Row 1: Sc in 2nd ch from hook and in each rem ch: 156 sc; ch 3 (counts as first dc of next row), turn.

Row 2: Dc in each sc, ch 3, turn.

Rows 3 and 4: Dc in each dc, ch 3, turn.

Row 5 (right side)**:** Dc in next 5 dc, work FC (see Special Sts) around next dc; *dc in top of same dc (working behind FC) and in next 11 dc, FC around next dc; rep from * to last 6 sts, dc in last 6 sts; ch 3, turn.

Row 6: Dc in next 5 dc, sk next FC; *dc in next 12 dc, sk next FC; rep from * to last 6 sts, dc in last 6 sts, ch 3, turn.

Rows 7 and 8: Dc in each dc, ch 3, turn.

Row 9: Dc in next 11 dc, work FC around next dc; *dc in same dc and in next 11 dc, work FC around next dc; rep from * to last 12 sts, dc in last 12 sts; ch 3, turn.

Row 10: Dc in next 11 dc, sk next FC; *dc in next 12 dc, sk next FC; rep from * to last 12 sts, dc in last 12 sts; ch 3, turn.

Rows 11 and 12: Dc in each dc, ch 3, turn.

Rep Rows 5 through 12 until piece measures about 50" long, ending by working a Row 6. At end of last row, turn, do not work ch-3.

Edging
Rnd 1: Ch 1, 3 sc in first st for corner; sc in each st to last st, 3 sc in last st for next corner; work sc evenly around entire piece, adjusting sts to keep work flat and working 3 sc in each outer corner, join with sc in beg sc.

Rnd 2: *Ch 3, sk next sc, sc in next sc; rep from * around, join. Finish off.

First Border
Hold piece with right side facing you and one short end at top; join yarn in first sc at upper right corner.

Row 1: Ch 5 (counts as a dc and ch-2 sp), dc in same sc; * (dc, ch 2, dc) in next ch-3 sp; (dc, ch 2, dc) in next sc; rep from * across, ch 5, turn.

Row 2: *Dc in next dc, ch 3, dc in next dc, ch 4; rep from * across, ending dc in last dc; finish off.

Second Border
Hold piece with right side facing you and other short end at top. Work as for First Border.